ALSO FROM TELLING OUR STORIES PRESS:

IMPACT: An Anthology of Short Memoirs

ROLL: A Collection of Personal Narratives

TURNS: A Collection of Memoir Chapbooks

*RESURRECTING PROUST: Unearthing
Personal Narratives through Journaling*

*THE BRIDGE: A Companion Journal for
Unearthing Personal Narratives and Memoir*

SO LONG: Short Memoirs of Loss and Remembrance

MEMOIR POETIC of a NAKED COP

MY CIA: A Memoir

REVERIE

Ultra Short Memoirs

REVERIE

Ultra Short Memoirs

Collected by

CoCo Harris

TELLING OUR STORIES PRESS

Telling the
Telling
Our
Stories of Our Lives
Press

Showcasing the Art of Literary Personal Narratives
Published by Telling Our Stories Press

The independent literary imprint with a focus on
the art of short memoir and personal narratives.

Requests for information should be forwarded to:
Telling Our Stories Press
www.TellingOurStoriesPress.com

Cover Art: REVERIE by Janine Lehane
Cover Design: Michael Milliken & CoCo Harris
Book Layout: Dafeenah Jameel of Indie Designz
A version of "Taking Daniel To The Baseball Den" by E. Ethelbert
Miller appeared in the Capital Community News, July 2013
Library of Congress Control Number: 2001012345

Printed in the United States of America
ISBN-13: 978-0-9900081-1-8
ISBN-10: 0990008118

This book is dedicated to my brand new angel,
my mother,

Gloria Jean Harris
(1940-2013)
whose ultra short memoir "Who Am I"
(that she allowed me to publish, and appeared in IMPACT: An
Anthology of Short Memoirs, 2012) inspired me in more ways
than one to continue to work with such short memoirs
which can pack so much story in so few words.
Her ultra short memoir taught me more about her "story"
and illuminated metaphors of her life's narrative
that I never knew existed...

Acknowledgements

I am thankful for all of the authors who have shared their narratives in these pages; and for Telling Our Stories Press Assistant Editor Nancy Prothro Arbuthnot, who is just always there.

I am ever grateful for my immediate family, George and the O-Girls, who endure my time away from the mix as I steal myself away to work and write and edit and work and write and edit.

CONTENTS

After all, all we have are our stories.

PEACE OF MINE

TAKING DANIEL TO THE BASEBALL DEN

E. Ethelbert Miller

Daniel my godson is six years old. He runs into Nationals Park ahead of me. Today is his first game, a baptism that will bless his life with playoffs and a World Series if he is lucky. I'm sixty-two and have never witnessed a no-hitter or a triple play. In 1965 I caught a ball in Yankee Stadium off the bat of Yankees back-up catcher Bill Bryan. On August 28, 2005, a ball hit by Jose Guillen dropped into my hands. What are the odds of being happy twice in life?

We arrive at the park an hour before the game starts. I take Daniel by the hand and we begin to walk around. When you attend a game with a child it's important to see the baseball universe through their eyes. Forget the pitch count—I have to take Daniel to the bathroom twice. During the 4th inning, seeking more food, we stand on a fast moving line. I can hear the action taking place on the field but I can't see anything. Does it matter?

What new faith have I introduced young Daniel to?

Tonight Daniel will fall asleep while wearing his baseball jersey. His mother will kiss him good night before leaving his room. How can a child dream without knowing baseball? How does a man remain forever young by simply watching the flight of a ball?

PICKING THROUGH POCKETS AND POCKETBOOKS
Don Segal

Stacks of papers to shuffle through,
Bags of bags of bags
And piles and piles and piles
Of clothes,
All so dusky in the dim
Cold darkness of the house.

Free samples of shampoo,
Hotel bars of soap,
Not just one or three or two
But dozens kept closeted with
Bags of candles dark with soot.

Unopened gifts, gloves and scarves
Linen tablecloths and towel sets,
Rolls of tape and tape and tape
Masking, electric and cellophane
To put every thing back together again.

Smallish boxes, cardboard and wood
Holding photographic lesions left in silver
Always happy smiling grinning.
How could the next moment have been
So harsh, remembered only with the tart

And pained scraping of bitter teeth
Behind pursed yet hollow searing lips.

Letters to Mother during the War,
Mothers Day cards made in school,
Fathers Day cards bought by children grown,
Tattered drawings by nieces too old to remember
What they drew or why,
Each face grinned so emphatically.

Suits contained the serious remains
Of funeral services, or graduations,
Funeral services and convocations,
Funeral services and weddings,
And funerals.

Dead leaved branches
Tattered and worn
Scraped against the windows
In the rain as I left.

STROKE
Leota McCown-Hoover

I wasn't a writer. I was a lecturer, a workshop facilitator. I spoke.

But all that changed one afternoon in 1988 when a small beige whale swam before my eyes; he didn't linger. Just one lap from left to right and out of sight, but he took with him many of my abilities. During the next six months he returned to swim more laps, each time he stole chunks of who I was. He wasn't a whale, of course, but a blood clot ripping and tearing through my brain's language center.

He stole my short-term memory; sentences became word lists without meaning. Lost, my ability to express myself verbally; gone, my spontaneity. Family and friends noticed these changes and were tolerant, all except my friend Gina.

She'd invited me for dinner and a sleepover. It was late, we were seated on the sofa, when without warning she snarled, "You're no longer a good friend. You're different. You always . . . you never." Stunned, I sat with tears dripping off my chin unable to speak. Gina, frustrated by my silence stomped off to bed.

I had no words. Not only no speech, but no words inside my head. Overwhelmed by emotion and a desire to explain, I searched her desk until I found pen and paper. Slowly, painfully, the pen found words. I explained. I apologized. I ended our friendship. I became a writer.

WAR AND BEAUTY
Lori Rottenberg

I am of two faces. My nose, the site of so many surgical battles, serves as a border between the two. One side, the victor, swaggers towards loveliness; it is the side presented for pictures, as if history did not exist. The other side sags, its defeated terrain marked by the shiny scar that spanned the original cleft. This is the side that knows the earlier truths, that remembers the wars and the hurts. Yet I'm finally done with this fighting: It's my special gift to learn from both beauty and ugliness, to see them for the veils they are.

You're So Beautiful

"You're so beautiful," he deadpanned, aiming his cruel turquoise eyes at the gawky 13-year-old bookworm with braces and a scarred face. I had surgery to correct a cleft lip at ages 3 months, 12, 17, and 25. It's still not right, but I'm done. Through luck and sweat, I now inhabit a fashionably lithe body; the books developed a good mind; the sadness shaped a heart that understands; and I've somehow achieved almost everything I wished for then. Maybe it's because I've learned that even though it's not the type of thing that shows up in pictures, he was right: I really am beautiful.

DIORAMA
Janine Lehane

The verandah is crested
with hanging plants: coleus
lavishly spinning a tale

for the glossy bromeliads,
laid at excellent intervals
on the planks that bear

baskets of macadamia nuts,
anodized milk tins,
a smart wireless radio,

and Granddad's red chair.
Inside, linoleum,
cool as you please,

the miracle of fruit flies
at the over-ripe mangoes,

Grandma's green chair—
for her back—with springs
and cushioning,

the Yardley talcum powder
and lady's perspiration
and resting in one's slip

on the green chenille
bedspread and Humpty,
forever surprised

according to
the Simplicity
pattern.

This is the rice
paper I walked,

tracing lines
accentuating, adjusting,

the bite of scissors
through cloth

and picking up
chores to aid
creative production

my feet on woolen
carpeting, elegant grey
with pink roses.

We all knew anticipation
and the dread
of interrupting

a dress, a cloak
a beautiful piece

and spinning

to show you
this new evidence:
this is joy

in pleats and tucks
and frills
and stitches

and lines
and joins
and drapes

and god-knows
how we'll get
it done in time,

flowing
and bunching
over polished wood,

miles of fabric
run across
the polished wood.

INTIMATE MEMOIRS
Gerald A. McBreen

I never visit
                    my father's grave
maybe that's why he visits me
or used to
not in many years now
The last time I was delivering mail
on upper Dogwood Street
in Auburn, Washington
He didn't say anything
I caught his shadow out of
the corner of my eye
When I turned to focus
he wasn't there
I started my trek again
there he was
in my peripheral vision
This time I didn't try to focus
I told him I wasn't ready to go
His attitude said
it was time to get ready
I have things I want to do
I said
but he was gone
I still have things
I want to do

EYES MEET
Michael Estabrook

One Friday night in the winter of 1971 I got the last seat on the bus home, back row in the middle, the worst seat. Sleet and snow turned the one hour ride into two.

The woman beside me fell asleep on my shoulder her name was Jean. We had spoken briefly over the months, so I knew she was 24 and worked at Fortunoff's in Manhattan. But mostly we'd simply say hi when our eyes would meet at the station.

She was tall, pretty and pleasant, with long brown hair. I liked her and watched her closely and could tell she hated men, especially middle-aged businessmen with plump wives and kids in college, making passes at her.

I never did that, never made passes, only said hi when our eyes would meet at the station. That was enough for me and she must've liked me too and trusted me because she never fell asleep on any other shoulder but mine.

THE NOTE
Gina Marie Lazar

Reading his note, I cringed. A tear fell from my cheek, smearing the ink on the page below.

"So long," it read. "I can finally be free. No more pain. It's the pain that's really killing me." The rest was illegible. But I knew what it said. He had told me before, many times: "If I leave this place, don't ever forget me. You're all I ever had."

And I knew he was going to do it—to fly away—someday. He was like the baby bird I had released as a child. My grandmother's words still lingered in the far reaches of my mind: "If you love something, let it go. If it comes back to you, it's yours. If it doesn't, it never was." So I let him fly away, knowing that he would not be coming back anytime soon.

I looked up at the sun. In my mind's eye, I pictured him smiling. And when it rained, the rain would be his tears.

The day they buried his ashes under the willowy roots and moist soil, beneath long shadows cast by the light of a full moon, they buried my heart. And the rain fell.

SURVIVOR
Bobbie S. Bryant

I am allergic to straw, hay, corn stalks, cedar trees, pollen, and animal dander. I live on a farm.

At five, I take a spill into the pig pen with three angry sows and their litters of pink piglets.

At 23, I launch a retail business, borrowing money at 22% interest. Seven years later, I sell out and make a small profit.

In torrential rain, I roll my car upside-down and walk away with only a scratch.

My boss's greed, excess spending, and poor judgment make front page headlines 276 times.

Breast cancer.

A cardiac cath.

Shingles.

Survivor.

FINDING PEACE
Jamie Johnson

From the time my daughter was conceived, I had pictured this perfect little being. Good grades, sports, the arts, and of course a caring soul, it was all part of my plan.

I lived that fairy-tale, until the day my eighteen-year-old daughter sat me down to tell me she was transgendered. She was a boy, and she needed a male body to match what she felt in her heart.

This was not part of my plan.

Panic.

Denial.

Fear.

Embarrassment.

Admittance.

Parents who are blindsided by an unthinkable parenting challenge seem to go through some strange twelve-step program. Realizing that many would not accept the realness of this condition, that discrimination and prejudice might always be part of our lives, made reaching that last peaceful place more difficult.

Somehow however, leaning on the shoulders of many, I arrived at the final two steps: acceptance and support.

Vanity almost made me forget the most critical part of being a parent: love.

X-ray vision would have helped during those really rough years. Years when I needed the clarity to see that it's what's inside, underneath what society judges... that's what's important.

I haven't lost a daughter. That soul that I loved to death is still in there. And I've gained a strong, levelheaded son of whom I am immensely proud.

THE VALUE OF LETTING GO
Casey Clabough

I have had, at times, more than my full share of the intellectual's arrogance. I am grateful to have expunged it. Part of what helped me do so was less an identification with my place and people and more a permanent associative merging with them. It remains an uneasy fellowship. I am attached to where I live but have never felt much at home there. It is a place where I possess responsibilities and burdens, and though they are part of who I am, I never truly feel myself until I am away, departed, somewhere. I used to will myself into attaining freedom through the powers of my mind, but my will or my mind, or both, are no longer powerful enough to do so.

I have learned to accept my surroundings while remaining at peace with myself. I ask no more of others than is within their power to give. I am no longer annoyed by their faults—to the point that my friends sometimes mistake my reaction for apathy. I have learnt to go my own way without bothering about what others may think of it. I demand freedom for myself and am willing to afford it to others. I have not found it impossible to laugh and shrug my shoulders when people act badly toward me. I have let go of my life and, in doing so, come to own it.

SPIRALS OF LIFE

FACTS NO FRILLS
Beth Lynn Clegg

brother lived eight hours
my arrival two years later
        bitterly disappointed father
                mother withdrawn
                        dysfunctional threesome
married at twenty
mother of three blessings
        daughter leslie
                son ted jr
                        son Patrick
divorced after thirty-one years
gainfully employed
        deposited first paycheck
                eventually
                        reconnected with
                                life-long friend
married again
        disaster
flying solo
terrific employment
        new horizons
son ted jr
        lost on California streets
                declared deceased
children
        in-law children

grandchildren
other family members
add joy to my life
as do friends
church activities
cooking
gardening
reading
two spoiled cats
making it easy to bloom where I'm planted

OMNI MUSING
W. Clayton Scott

here I long

to live

for the future

but talk

in past tense

of what

happened then

that is

now forever

Mini Memoir
William L. Janes

Born from ancient watered-down royalty into modest lower middle classness; comfortably destined to some mediocre greatness but taking the low road instead. Diving under the gutter to spend life with Jim, Jack, Johnny, and all their 80-proof friends. Smoking anything that held a flame and snorting what didn't. Pinpricks, cages and a nodding acquaintance with death as friends dropped like mercury in winter. Marriage, children, white picket fences taken by The Man or smothered by the Monster.

Done.

Sudden lucidity at the end of a fist. Slow motion suicide replaced by a sense of purpose and the love of a South American angel.

Life anew.

HOME CAME TO ME
Emily Fraser Voigt

My ex-pat Venezuelan early-childhood was full of fun and swimming and piñatas. Then we headed "home", to gray, wet England, where my experiences made me feel alien. Time and again, I failed to connect with my peers, coming across as too pretentious. Stuck-up. Weird. Bad choices as a teenager ensued.

After college, I bounced from country to country like a hollow ping-pong ball on a wooden floor. Click, click, clickety-click. Light as a feather: the pauses between each bounce getting smaller and smaller. I taught English; waited tables; worked as a translator. I continued to make a few bad choices.

Until I met Patrick.
He got me.
He cherished me.
He treated me with respect.
He gave me a foundation.

Together, we moved around a lot, but I had more of a sense of belonging than I ever had before. Then Elliot came along, and suddenly I don't want to move any more at all. My beautiful, blue-eyed, smiley boy has changed my perspective on everything. I still don't know where I'll live two years from now, but I will always be his mother and that permanence has made me feel that at last, I have a home. The ball has come to rest.

LITTLE WIND
Elaine Dugas Shea

From type on a folded Western Union
Telegram yellow and pumpkin stained,
I was first-born in wartime and grew
Like a poppy bright orange and fragile.
My beloved younger brother Al
Demonstrated life skills artfully,
And seemed so much older.
A water nixie, I swam in the Atlantic, hiked
New England hills and taught young children.
My community expanded into volunteer service
As a civil rights worker in the rural south,
A pivotal moment in our nation's history.
This advocacy ribboned through my life with
Migrant Farm workers and American Indian Tribes—
Continuing today, friendship never lost or far away.

THE BEST GIRL
Ashley Henley

Born pale and silent with something to prove in white-hot Florida heat. Only child of two PhDs. Wide-eyed pilgrimage to DC ("Job opportunities"). Found snow falling like heavy ash and people moving fast. Big yellow house among big yellow houses. Round and round on training wheels with sticky hands and scraped knees. Papers marked Satisfactory, forced half-smiles. I WANT TO BE THE BEST GIRL IN SCHOOL written neatly in a journal. Expectations. Burgeoning perfectionism. Building and building, combusting in forceful, roaring defiance. Drugs, sex, chipped black nail polish. Fleeting abandon. State university and The Return of The Perfection. Anxiety, mediocrity, love, loss, love, loss, serotonin reuptake inhibitor. Love like pious worship. Life-sustaining love. Marriage. Old brick house, yellowed wood, barking, sweeping piles of dogwood petals falling like heavy ash. Ambition—fierce, bellowing ambition. So many expectations. Sleek black slacks, smart blouses, loud necklaces that scream I'M NOT LIKE YOU. Promotions, committees, big glass buildings. I WANT TO BE THE BEST GIRL. Quiet, torpid traffic, endless radio chattering. Arriving home, pale, silent, and with something to prove.

BIGGER SKIN
Jean Bonin

There was a child I used to know

She did not ask if she could go

She just put on some bigger skin

Then hand in hand

Walked away

With him

I begged the child

To stay a while

But she left

Me breathless

In grown up style

Then the child I knew

Knew me no more

She turned the key

In future's door

The child I knew faded away

Into the mist of yesterday

Sometimes I think I see her still

She invades my memory

At her will

Then silently she slips away

Back into the shadow of yesterday

STRENGTH
Valerie D. Benko

In silence, she watched her twin die before leaving the womb. Somehow she survived and they named her Valerie – which meant strength. She'd need it for the life she would lead. Her father was an abusive alcoholic; her mother fled to safety and left her behind. She played dumb to survive. In college, she broke her neck in a car accident. Doctors said she shouldn't have lived, but she did. Before she turned thirty, she was diagnosed with multiple sclerosis. The disease threatens to end her career and statistics show she could die early. But she'll survive.

VACATION IN VUNG TAU
Pavelle Wesser

Saigon, Vietnam—1969

At three, my mother moved me to the war zone to be closer to my father, who was operating on injured patients. We lived in hospital housing where I feasted on food like Spam, something you now receive via e-mail.

"See how lucky you are!" my mother pointed to mutilated children in the hospital hallways as in a daze, I sucked my thumb. It was the one thing I could count on, even though she threatened to cut it off.

Running errands with her one day, the air raids sounded, and we sought shelter inside a shop. While my mother paced, I explored the aisles, sliding open a cabinet to find myself face to face with a terrified woman clutching her son to her chest.

"You are the enemy," her eyes accused.

I ran to my mother. "Momma, there's a …"

"Let's go." Grabbing my hand, she marched me down the scorching streets.

We ended our stay with a seaside vacation in Vung Tau, where jellyfish stung my legs and prostitutes pursed their painted lips at my tears.

"It was off-season," my mother shook her head, "your father was confused."

As was I, judging by the twisted images that played in bizarre succession in my mind.

"Death is too morbid for children," my mother concurred on the way back home.

I nodded through the ringing in my ears.

New York City—1975

"Why does your father perform transsexual surgery?" the kids would ask.

I might have answered: "He got a head start on soldiers whose testicles had been blown apart stepping on landmines," but frankly, it never even occurred to me.

"You're weird!"

By the time they delivered their verdict, I'd ceased listening as voices chattered mindlessly within the depths of tortured dreams.

THEN
Bobbie Hayse

We were too high to know we'd had too much, and too fucked up to even care. Our days ran away like wild horses over the hills, and we were the only ones to blame.

Some days we would spend in the car all-day driving to pain clinics somewhere south of the state line. Their parking lots were filled with out-of-state plates, Mercedes Benz, Jaguars.

"Pillbillies Go Home" billboards along the interstate read.

And still we would ride: sponsor, driver, addict, the afflicted.

TRUTH AND BEAUTY
Diane Caldwell

Running away from home at the age of 16 set the tone of my life. Hopping a Trailways Bus to New York City in search of "Truth" and "Beauty." Finding 'truth" in the jagged smiles of New York's lower east side's street people. Lessons in shoplifting. Begging. Learning how to share everything. And tasting undiluted freedom. Panhandling for beer money. Walking up to the second level of Tad's Steaks and scarfing down the remains of discarded dinners. Weren't those abandoned baked potato skins the tastiest bites of food ever eaten?

What can I say? After you've been a beggar—the thing most people fear more than anything—you know you can survive anything. Not just survive, but live. Thrive. Delirious moments sitting on sun-licked benches in Thompson Square Park next to Ellen Kennedy and Jimmy the Greek, Pat De Vita and William Thomas Quinn. No pretense. No status. Just the free-wheeling moment.

And so even today, it's the alternative side of the street where I feel most comfortable. Among the dawn's crazy rag-tag humanity. Sharing a cup of coffee with roaming, soul-eyed misfits in the ragged reality of a sun rise wink.

TOUCHSTONE
Helen Carson

Three days of peace and music
Touchstone of an era
Pot smokers, bra burners made
Love while the white dove sang...
on a farm called Woodstock

World away no music played
Along the Ho Chi Minh Trail
Where bloodied soldiers fell
Stench of fear filled the air...
in a place called Vietnam

Rich vein of inner crazy
Divided generation that
Summer of love and war
We have outlived that day...
and come safely home

LIES WE TELL
OURSELVES
AND OTHERS

LUCIDITY
Catherine Lee

We never talk about it, that day of shatterings
In the hospital when grandma's long goodbye
Lifted in a momentary frenzy of truth,
As if the bellows of her soul could not sustain
The heaviness of silent years, the friction of life
Meeting death inside her mind forcing breath
To form into words never spoken.

Her fractious lucidity broke through
The soil of her mind to splinter family trees.
She spoke of a secret day when he came
Across the Pacific in his wrinkled uniform
To be all that he could be, but you said no
In a language he didn't hear, screamed it
For your husband and your sons.

Our homogeneous blood diluted in a day,
Answering the question-mark hook
That always snagged the back of my mind,
Explaining the lingering pain of two generations,
The lightness of my hair that should have been
Black as the coal tears smudged beneath your eyes,
Black as the heart of a man I hate, but yearn to know.

NOT YET
OR THE FOLLOW-UP VISIT
Jasminne Mendez

I sat in a grey chair, wearing a grey dress surrounded by purple walls and a room full of women. I had taken my pills that morning on an empty stomach. That was a mistake. I felt stoned. They called my name. I signed in and paid the $25 copay. I held my purse close; it was the only thing I was certain of. I texted my husband and told him I was expecting the worst. He told me to call him when it was all over. "All over, all over," I repeated in my head. As if it wasn't already.

I looked around the room; there were four women bursting with life at the seams and me. I clutched my purse to my empty stomach. I felt lost. But the eyes and smile of a four-year-old girl found me. She walked towards me with a magazine in her hands. She set it down and began to point at the pictures. She pointed to things she didn't know the names of and I gave them a name.

"That's a penny. That's a key, a lock, a…"

"A MONKEY!" She yelled.

"Yes, that's right." I smiled unwillingly. "How old are you?" I asked.

She shrugged.

"Are you five?"

"No."

"Are you four?"

"Yes. Why are you here?" She asked me innocently.

"I'm here to see the doctor," I said.

"Oh. Why?"

"Just to make sure I'm healthy again."

"Oh. Is there a baby in your tummy too?"

I paused. "No. Not yet," I said.

"Oh." And we smiled to break the tension.

Not yet. I had lied and said, not yet. But the truth was: not anymore.

CALL YOU IN THE MORNING
Adam Cheshire

Drunk, I leave my girlfriend's house and drive to the gay bar.

The front door is locked, a proudly self-aware plaque screwed into its wood: "After 10pm, enter in back."

At the bar, I watch the ebullient boys on the dance floor, shake with a subtle sense of liberation, and wonder what the fuck I'm doing here.   Searching for the doppelganger of an adolescent crush, perhaps, an echo made flesh.

There's no guilt. This is merely a self-administered psychological trial; a measurement of lust. I don't know if I want any of them, really, never having fully acknowledged such desire. I'm not gay, after all.

But over there, conversing with the lithe, indistinguishable forms, a reminiscence stirred in his wide, insouciant grin; a slim cheek in the shadows like a certain cool young sleeping face.

I've been staring too long. A man sitting across the bar looks at me and laughs, dirty and pitiful.

Stumbling out the back of the bar, my legs still staticky with lingering music, I ease into a stride, the air soothing, the night black with discovery.

THE SIGHTING
Jessica Heriot

The leaves are always dry on the cobblestones around the Hayden Planetarium. They crisp and crunch underfoot. Leon didn't know why he was there, so uncharacteristic to leave work in the middle of the day, but he had a child urge to sit in the dark planetarium, look up at the black dome sky, and listen to a soothing voice describe the constellations.

The auditorium was half filled, groups of school kids and scattered adults, mostly old people, some with grandchildren. While scanning the dim lit room, he spotted him. It can't be, he thought. But it was, the nose, the sad eyes like his own, wispy gray hair covering a wide bald spot. And the woman…He didn't want to look, but he did. Her hand rested on his leg.

Shock, embarrassment, disappointment rushed in all at once. So, pop found a woman to be with. He understood. Silent long-suffering Harry, enduring years of his wife's affair with a judge named Solomon of all things. No secret, everyone knew. She had packed her bags many times, creating havoc in their home life for years. Good for him, he thought.

Was there ever any love or attraction between them he wondered? No, an arrangement of necessity. She was sixteen. His birth closed the door, sealed their fate. He got up, took one quick look at his father and the woman, and slipped out.

CUT THE TANGLES OUT
Missi Smith

"Did you cut your hair?"

"No?" I avoided eye contact. I grew up Lutheran and Jesus was always watching at our house. His voyeurism worked on my conscience and at eight years old, this was absolutely the first time I had ever lied to my mom. However, moms know. They always know. I got spanked that day.

"I'm not angry because you cut your hair, Missi. I'm angry because you lied to me when I asked you about it," my mom explained after the spanking that "hurt Mom more than it hurt Missi."

I learned my lesson about lying when I was eight and I never did it again; however, when I was seventeen, my parents changed the rules and my family members and I began an intricate series of lies and deception that would lead me long into adulthood.

I was seventeen, my niece was two, and my sister was in jail. "We're adopting her," my mom announced to me. "Ayrelle will be your sister and she will not know any different. She will not know Sam is her mom and that we are her grandparents. We are her parents now as far as we're concerned."

The reality of what my mom told me scared me fiercely because I realized she was already in the process of weaving a whole new history for Ayrelle. This was not a negotiation. How in the world did they think this could work?

Just like I cut away the tangled mass of hair, we were going to chop away two years of the past and create a whole new reality for one little girl. I was going to learn to live a lie. I hoped Jesus really was watching us now.

SORROW'S DOOR

THE DEATH OF A CHINESE WIDOW
(for Li Juying)
Changming Yuan

In a remote Chinese village
On a forgotten winter night
A 38-year-old poor woman
Tried hard to sit up noiselessly
Put aside rather than on her padded clothes
Crawled out of her frameless bed
And resolutely drowned herself
In a broken wide-brimmed water jug

Behind herself she left neither worth nor words
Except three teenagers who had been
Bullied and looked at with slanting white eyes
By their fellow villagers
(who bore the same family name)
Ever since their father died
Of an untreated disease
13 years before

Years later, her children understood
Why she killed herself
In a water jug on that night
Many years after she had been suffering
From a painful
But not fatal disease

Years later, her only son told me
Why my grandma
Chose to drown herself almost naked
On that cold night

NOODLE-MINING
Jean Butterfield

When I walked into the kitchen my mother was at the sink doing dishes. Her upturned face leaned into the cool evening light from the window above the sink, ecstatic with some soundless fervent prayer. Her eyes pressed firmly closed, circling around an ever-inward diving thought. Her hands immersed in soapy water, thick with foam, fingers groping in the deep. What was she looking for? Was she longing for something, noodle-mining for that last hard baked piece at the bottom? When had she become invisible? Why had I never looked the thousand times she cleaned, mended, glued together the puzzle of broken pieces over and over again. How had I not been witness?

MY MOTHER'S HANDBAG
Stephanie C. Horton

Bright West African moonlight bathes the white marble graves in the churchyard across the street opposite my bedroom window. The yellow curtains are halfway open. My small green plastic suitcase is packed beside me. I am eleven years old living this night ritual waiting for my mother to come for me. I finally fall asleep dreaming my cheek is resting against my mother's fragrant arm. I memory-dream hitting my father's fists with my mother's high-heeled shoe. I memory-dream mothering my mother, cradling her head in my lap, patting her to quiet her terrible sobs while my tears drip on her hair. My mother's friends jokingly called me her handbag because she took me with her wherever she went. I cannot imagine she will accept the law that tore me from her for daring to plead and win her case for a divorce. I wait for my mother to kidnap me and flee to some faraway country. I cannot understand how she could possibly be happy without me by her side. She marries again two years later. Her new husband's four young daughters are now her daughters. When I become a mother, I grow to understand how a mother's love holds surrender. I grow to understand why my motherland Liberia bleeds at war, ruled by brutal warlords and violent foreign mercenaries. I am an exile thirty-one years in America when my mother comes to see the doctor. Terminal cancer. I never leave her side. And of my mother's five belly-born children and the four she raised, I alone am in the house beside her when death comes. My eyes hold hers until hers dim to close forever forty-three years after that first killing separation. I am my mother's handbag. I cross an ocean to carry my mother home.

AFTER THE DEATH OF INFANT TWINS
Carol Kanter

The universe conspires
So everything reminds of this loss
Of what's no longer here
Or possible

Not just the sight of a double stroller
Twice anything

But one baby is enough.

A sand castle
Clowns with balloons
Balloons (sans clowns), kites
Fun in any form

Pimento-stuffed olives
The Harvest moon
Any glass—empty, half-empty, or full
Gladioli
The color blue
The Unbearable Lightness of Being
Dali's limp watches
Bracelets, bonnets, blankets

A bedtime tune, music
Bedtime

That ravenous wolf
Undeserving step-mothers
General Hospital
Doctors—Spock, Welby, Zhivago, Seuss

Live wires
Sky, the Milky Way, a chilly sun
Birds

Birthdays, holidays, the Sabbath
The month Grandpa died
Tsunamis
Other tragedies our minds cannot fathom
Philosophy, recorded history
E=m(c squared)
The fall
Summer, winter, spring.
"Fair."

SHENANDOAH
Sally Zakariya

I who did not trust canoes trusted
you to paddle me across to the cave
where the buzzards nested,
but I wasn't there the day
you went too close to the dam
with its rush and suck of water
and the boat went over and
the young girl went in, into that
ominous swirl.

O Shenandoah I love your waters,
they sing, Away, I'm bound away,
and in saving her you were bound away,
down to the concrete face of the dam,
pressed hard by the weight of the water
as it pushed to get through the narrow
steel grate, and you crossed over to the
other side of life.

Years later my new husband lost
his wedding ring in the muddy shallows
downstream from the dam
and dove and dove for it
as if to prove his love
and on the shore I prayed as hard
as a lapsed Episcopalian can
that the lovely waters wouldn't take
another love away.

I'M SICK; THEREFORE I AM
Beatriz Badikian-Gartler

They say asthma is the fear of losing your mother.
Unable to breathe—at 5 or 6
or 8—I'd call on all the neighbors to surround me
and scare death away. At night
I'd sit up on my narrow bed and gasp
and choke, trying to suck some crumbs of oxygen out of
the sad air, to fill my crowded lungs, and stay alive one more
day. Drowning in this manner became routine,
one more desperate fact of life in that home,
where disease gave us a reason for living.

Falling,
falling,
never landing quite gracefully. When I was young
(and even now)
I'd fall often,
trip first, fall later actually,
because of my bad leg,
my bad foot actually. Polio plucked a muscle out of
my right leg, the one from your knee to your big toe,
left the right foot with little control,
less power.
Unable to bend my ankle upward, the foot falls
Downward—a head bent over disconsolate and glum,
the red hibiscus spent and dried. It catches on carpets
and rugs, on raised sidewalks, stumbles and falls,

one leg in front, good and strong, the other
behind, useless as an afterthought.

Sinking,
sinking,
I sink into the vertiginous black hole and disappear
from the mirror's returning gaze, swallowed up
in one
swift
gulp.
It always happens this way:
sudden and inevitable
like a plane crash, the phone ring,
the summer shower.
Where do these ghosts come from and
how do they find me?

GAS
Evelyn Lampart

Upon descending the stoop stairs with my baby brother's stroller, my mother turned to tie a kerchief under my chin. It was too tight I told her. She didn't want me to catch a cold, she said. We were headed to Pitkin Avenue window-shopping.

After we had taken a few steps my mother instructed me to go back upstairs to our apartment, and check on the gas. Was it turned off? She didn't remember, and wanted to be sure. I went back alone. Our apartment was peaceful and still and the kitchen stove was at rest.

My mother did this every time we went window shopping. She was a young girl in Russia when our people were being gassed by the Nazis.

APARTMENT BUSINESS
SueAnn Porter

Emma had forgotten to buy beer for Fred for the last time. "Bam!" A bullet rushed through the barrel of the gun and hit Emma in the face.

Neighbors confessed that they often heard Fred and Emma arguing, but they decided to mind their own business.

But my father was the one who cleaned the mess off the walls. You see, my parents owned the apartment building. It was their business.

And my mother was the one who wrote the classified ad for the newspaper.

I was the one who explained to callers, "Yes, it's a one-bedroom apartment. FRESHLY PAINTED."

DESPERATION
Diana Raab

it is 2 a.m. and I am still awake rolling in my thoughts—tears rise from beneath smudged makeup and wrinkle cream which has not yet earned its keep as my mind stumbles to find a rhyme while i tremble in memories and wonders of futures and why some days rain with dismal thoughts and others pour sunshine like evening, when car beams paralyze roaming deer as i snatch a whiff of the loneliness which engulfs me during this dreary month of December; so much to be thankful for, but those sentiments do not sing to me now as the birds hover and my puppy is sprawled upon bunion infested feet oblivious to the past meshed with joy and pain and shaken from a missed father long gone and a mother who barely hears my words when i ask release from my own mind's prison which holds peace that once knocked on my front door whispering words of condolence, but what message do i need to hear to believe good words while my crazy mind holds on with delicate fingertips to life's ledge wanting to be saved by unknowns or perhaps this light green pillowcase offers elusive answers...

...I know it will be okay. let me find lust. let me wear a smile. i don't predict futures

...i just want to make them happen ...

NEW DECK PLEASE
Jean Horak

I was always told that you had to work with the cards dealt to you...good thing I had some hiding up my sleeve. I look into the room where my entire family sleeps on the floor and smile even though I am about to walk into the room across the hall where I let a man have his way with my young body. It's no matter though, not until I come home and realize that my mother is not sleeping on the floor, but has finally died from the disease taking over her body and soul. Out another door I go and into a new house. Stealing, lying, drugs, deceit...gotta love family. Life swirls by in a succession of folded cards and new deals. I am finally 18 and think I am on my own (no chance). Walk through a new door and see my father's cancer ravaged body. When the recognition leaves his eyes for good, I walk out of the hospital door and never see him again. Life goes on, the best we can do is keep replacing the cards we were dealt.

PORTRAITS WE PAINT OF OURSELVES AND OTHERS

WATER ISLAND DAYS
Richard Goodman

The summer of 1978 we spent on Water Island, a small enclave of houses just thirty miles from New York City on the ocean.

All of us there, on a late Sunday morning, in sandy liberation on the beach. The happiness of being with these people, with Nancy and Bruce, with Kerri, waiting for Pamela, who always slept late.

"Well. Looks like mauve is the color for fall." Nancy said, pausing with her flipping and examining a page of *Vogue*.

I loved Nancy with her retinue of suntan lotions, magazines, floppy hat, how she sat back and crossed her legs and flipped her magazine pages like she was watching a parade, each page a different float. She wore her glasses deep in her hair.

"Not again," Kerri said.

I loved Kerri, with his pale, trim body, his wit, his searching for humor anywhere he could find it. He had light, springy curly hair, cut short, a wide smile and an irresistible staccato laugh.

"Some of these sweaters are yummy," Nancy said. "Why aren't you less expensive?" She looked up at Bruce as if he could change the prices.

"Richard, I think she's talking to you," Bruce said.

I loved Bruce with his bone-dry comments, his fearlessness. He was from Connecticut, had grown up privileged, but never exploited that in any way. He had a way of tilting his head upward, slightly to one side, when he was making a comment, usually something memorably witty.

About an hour or so later, we heard someone behind us, approaching. We craned our necks, and there she was, Pamela, in her one-piece bathing suit, hauling a beach chair in the most ungainly way, trudging toward us.

Now the group was complete.

DISCOVERY
Meredith Hoffman

Discovery.
You eat enchiladas under mini Mayan gods and
I watch you shave your head, flex angry muscles and play chess in
a Washington jail seven years ago.
You're the man in the red flannel across the restaurant table,
The one I would've approached were I not with you
I collage together your Safeway nightshifts as a teen your fist-
ready father your comedy scripts killing me in laughs your grip of
me naked upside down,
a body,
just a body,
half your size.
No wonder you're so convincing.
We make it a policy to stay alone,
Whether it's an artist thing or 21st century New York thing I
can't answer
Nor care to
But remember
I'm not to flinch if I never hear from you tomorrow.

TRAIN BIRTH
Diane Spodarek

I was born in motion
The train rocking and surging
Metal against metal
I popped out on a double seat
in a little town called Puce,
which is French for flea -
or so they tell me -
Fifteen miles east of Windsor, Ontario
Canada.

Water blood afterbirth
And my mother's tears
Mixed with clapping and cheering
and a champagne toast.
Some fell on me.
And at birth,
I was already moving
and drinking

SWEET JOY
Nancy Prothro Arbuthnot

FIRST BORN

June 3: due date for our first child. Awakened by contractions, I send Stephen to work, call my father. He'd participated, vicariously, in the births of seven children (if "vicarious" could include the time he landed his Banshee at Guantanamo and heard of my birth) and coaxes me through contractions. In the afternoon, my mother drives me to my appointment. Is this your first? the doctor asks. Then you have time. At the hospital, I feel a stab of emptiness as I wave good-bye to my mother. I lean on Stephen's arm, suddenly terrified. Couldn't this baby just stay inside?

MANCHILD

What did I, oldest of six sisters, know of boys? How could I raise a son? We named Charles after his grandfather, named for his father, Charles William. The doctor tied off the extra fingerling—a little knob remains, reminding him of the luck he carries. Still also faintly visible on his cheek are two tiny parallel scars, a gift from Margaret, twenty-two months, who leaned to kiss him, we thought, then carved the blossoming tulip-stems on his face. Then in a clear, bell-like voice, she spoke her longest sentence ever—I want to hold the baby.

CADETTE

Her name's Annie, I tell Stephen as she slips out, red-haired, howling, Anne with an "e," in case we go to France. Then I gobble down my surf and turf dinner. Then I fall asleep.

Was she a mistake? a colleague whispers when I show up, Annie in arms. I post Ben Jonson's lament on the bulletin board outside my office: Here lies my best piece of poetry. I'm taking a semester's leave. It would be too crazy to get up at 5 a.m., settle three children into the car to drive to Annapolis. It's time to think of something new.

WHITE OUT
Carmen Gillespie

"A weather condition caused by a heavy cloud cover over the snow, in which the light coming from above is approximately equal to the light reflected from below, and which is characterized by absence of shadow, invisibility of the horizon, and discernibility of only very dark objects."

I remembered white outs from the Little House books, people losing orientation from barn to house, unable to find their home, six-feet away. But this was my house, enveloped by billows of white so opaque that even inside we felt adrift—the house, me, my husband, and my daughters (one a teen-ager, the other still becoming inside me) unmoored. The windows were paper-blank white and illuminated, reversing but mirroring, like a photographic negative, night's indeterminate dark. My husband wanted to go out and be in the middle of that lost. I did not let him. Even so, he was lost.

THE BLUES
Ellen Dworsky

After three years, I have few tangible items to remember him by. A ticket stub from one of the two movies we saw in the theater, a few CDs he burned with songs he knew I'd like, a DVD of a sci-fi movie he wrote and filmed, a red fabric rose he picked up at a gas station as a belated birthday present. And a mustard yellow and orange colored God's eye—the kind you make with yarn and Popsicle sticks.

We were on our way back to Albuquerque after a weekend in Cimarron and had stopped for gas in Wagon Mound. The man behind the counter gave him the God's eye instead of change. He presented it to me when he got back in the car after paying for the gas. It's still in my glove box.

But there have been two gifts he's given me I will never forget even though I can't hold them in my hands. Last Christmas, surprised that I had gotten him a Christmas present—though I always give him presents, especially for his birthday and Christmas—he realized he'd have to get me something.

"What do you want?" he asked. I said,

"Something that says you know me. It doesn't have to be something you buy."

So he took the lyrics to the first song I'd ever written—a blues song—and put them to music. Drums, bass, guitar. He even learned slide guitar, a style he'd never played before but learned because he knew I loved it. He sang the lyrics I had written, adding a few lines of his own. And he gave my untitled song a name: "Got Those Leavin' You Blues."

What he never knew was that when I wrote that song, I was thinking of him.

CONVERSATION WITH MY FATHER
Aileen R. McCready

"Daddy, do you want to change your shirt?"

"Why?"

"You wore it yesterday."

"It's clean."

"Why don't you wear the shirt Joseph gave you for Father's Day?"

"I didn't even know it was Father's Day. Did you give me a sweater?"

"Five years ago. Do you want to take a shower?"

"No."

I want to run away and never come back.

"Let me help you change your shirt."

"It looks bad?"

"I just thought you'd wear your new one."

"Who gave me that?"

"Joseph."

"That's right. I'm lucky you're here to take care of me."

I want to stay forever.

FRAMED PHOTOGRAPH OF YOUR FATHER
Judith Serin

Your mother kept it by her bedside and you take it home when she dies. You're sure she didn't recognize him the last years of her life. Even a few years before, when she still talked to you, she told you she'd been thinking about "him." "Who?" you asked. "Him." She pointed to the photo, your father's name already lost.

This is not the most handsome picture of your father. His face is fleshy, but the skin is firm, the only wrinkles the fine lines across his forehead, both horizontal and vertical; and the deep crimps around his eyes. Behind the dark-rimmed glasses his eyes are almost closed with the depth of his smile. The lines under his cheeks are the same as the ones your mother had, you and your sister have now. His collar is open; there's a hint of stubble on his chin.

He's just there, unselfconscious as your sister sometimes is in photos and your mother and you never are. In that moment genuinely enjoying whatever is there, as in another moment he might have been angry or so sunk in thought that the world vanished.

Eight years after he died you were in the bathtub. You heard a trumpet play six notes. Then felt him right there with you.

ELAPSED
Callie Melton

My mother, always crunching
With her hand in a cup of ice
Fishing for the suspended stinging molecules with
Thick yellow nails
And
Peanuts in her coke
And
Pistachios
Always crunching and cracking and chewing
My bones in the innards of her round face that I dislike because I
    have it too
Then cackling through broad stained teeth at
My step-father, who is always mending
With his weary tattooed and sun spotted hands
That are faded like the memories of the oriental waters they once
    parted
And the M14 they once cradled
Now knotted with arthritis and
Kneading strips of leather as he mumbles his intentions through
    a jaw of brown mint spew
Smiling shrewdly with his eyes
At how my mother was a city baby when he found her
As was I, and my sister
Though according to him,
I have the most sense
Bitter smells of summer polk-boiling Steam

Winters battle for warmth- Kerosene
And now I smell the
Decaying wood of antiques and my infancy and the old house
Beneath this one, hidden and buried when everything was
    renewed
And reconstructed, the pre-fab home and
My mother's womb by his son and
Her crunching, crunching, for nine months
After which the babies were no longer babies and
My sister got lost in the world, in search of love
And I became a portrait

THE MOUSE HOUSE
Kathy Gilbert

For Julie, my microbiologist mother
Art Deco Buffalo City Hall, 21st floor
in your white lab coat you peer through an oil
immersion microscope for parasites:
cryptosporidium, schistosomes, filaria, leishmania.

You pause, stand, and gaze out: Lake Erie
iron grey with a winter storm coming,
look towards Black Rock and the lighthouse.

Cynthia, colleague and cohort, a friendly
face in a sea of men, comes in from the Milk
and Water Lab. Her next vacation plan:
a tramp freighter to Egypt on the Nile.

You, who have traveled from the farm in Alberta
to the States; from Depression to Recession;
from daughter, to mother; nowhere else, are envious.

Now a dog's skull to open, a brain to dissect
slicing tissue samples of Negri bodies; prepping
injections for the mice to detect rabies.

You open the door to a closet full of cages.
Mice, hundreds, some with picric yellow painted stripes
indicating they were injected, squeak; the rancid odor,
fetid smell of rodent fur, pours into your nostrils.

Later you will bring one mouse home to me, your
sixteen year old daughter, to chloroform, cut,
extract the heart, keeping it beating with a salt solution
on the kitchen table. You want me to be a surgeon.

Scalpel in shaking hand, I realize I don't have
eyesight or steadiness to fulfill that dream; but
with you in mind, I will see rivers of five continents.

BE GONE
Marilyn June Janson

"Now I know what it will feel like when I'm terminal," Mom says.

I pretend not to hear her.

In our Miami hotel room I'm watching Sue Ellen and J.R. Ewing fight on Dallas. On spring break from college Mom took me on vacation.

Without my dad.

"Poor Betty Bacall," my mother continues. "Bogart suffered so much before cancer took his life."

I am sorry I gave her Lauren Bacall's autobiography to read.

At least Lauren was there for Bogy.

Mom had ovarian cancer. Three years later she was terminal.

She died alone.

Dad chose to be gone.

CONTRIBUTORS

NANCY PROTHRO ARBUTHNOT is a poet and Professor Emerita of English at the United States Naval Academy. Her publications include *Guiding Lights: United States Naval Academy Monuments and Memorials* (Naval Institute Press); *Wild Washington: Animal Sculptures A to Z* (The Annapolis Publishing Company), with Cathy Abramson; and *From Where the Wind Blows* (Vietnamese International Poetry Society), with Le Pham Le. *Spirit Hovering*, a collection of meditative lyric poems, is being published by Tate Publishing in 2014.

BEATRIZ BADIKIAN-GARTLER was born and reared in Buenos Aires, Argentina, and has lived in the Chicago area for over thirty-five years. Badikian-Gartler holds a Ph.D. in English from the University of Illinois at Chicago and teaches at various institutions of higher learning. Her essays, poems, and stories have been published in numerous journals, anthologies, and newspapers in the United States and abroad. She is a popular performer in the Chicago area and lectures often on women's issues, art, and literature. In 2000 Badikian was selected as one of the One-Hundred Women Who Make a Difference in Chicago by *Today's Woman* magazine. She is an Illinois Humanities Council Road Scholar and a frequent Newberry Library instructor. Her second full length collection, *Mapmaker Revisited: New and Selected Poems*, was published in 1999 from

Gladsome Books in Chicago. Her first *novel Old Gloves—A 20th Century Saga* was published in 2005 by Fractal Edge Press in Chicago. Her artwork has been exhibited at Robert Morris College, Around the Coyote art festival, and other venues in Chicago. Her collages are available for purchase on her website: www.bbgartler.com.

VALERIE D. BENKO is a thriving writer from Western Pennsylvania where she works full-time as a Communications Specialist.

JEAN BONIN and her husband run a small horse boarding and training facility on the beautiful Alberta prairies where they enjoy both the sunshine and the snow, often on the same day. Jean has always enjoyed stories and poems from both sides of the ink. Sunshine or snow Jean can be found either in the saddle or curled around her computer writing. Over the years she has had several short stories, devotionals and poems published.

BOBBIE S. BRYANT is a native Kentuckian currently residing in Louisville. She provides marketing and promotional assistance, as well as historic and genealogical research, to Smith Farms, her family's ten-generation tobacco farm in Calloway County. She also hosted a daily morning television show and a monthly broadcast featuring notable people of Western Kentucky. Most recently, Bobbie served as associate producer of *Farming in the Black Patch*, a PBS documentary currently airing on KET. Her recently published works include 'Life in the Black Patch," (*The Courier Journal*, February, 2013), *Passions of the Black Patch: Cooking and Quilting in Western Kentucky* (2012), "Kentucky Kindness," (*Underwired Magazine*, April 2012), *Forty Acres & A Red Belly Ford: The Smith Family of Calloway County*, (2011), "The Five Virtues of Mollie," (*Underwired Magazine,* September

2011), "The Badge," (*Clay County Ancestral News Magazine*, 2011); and "The Comfort of Home," was the winner of the 2010 Bluegrass Literacy Fall Writing Contest.

JEAN BUTTERFIELD works in the San Francisco Bay Area as a freelance illustrator and designer for independent publishers, and creates promotional materials for regional theatre companies. Several of her self-authored, hand-typeset, hand-bound books have been exhibited in California and Arizona. Her plays have been performed with *Berkeley Rep Theatre Playwriting Workshop, Ross Alternative Works in Marin, Cue Live in Concord*, and as a winner of Reverie Productions' Next Generation Playwriting Contest in New York City.

DIANE CALDWELL now lives in Istanbul and occasionally writes about her life. Almost 10 years ago, stifling sobs, she boarded a plane to Greece and hasn't been back to the states since. Running away from home at age 16 and fleeing to New York in search of "Truth and Beauty," set the tone for her life. She's danced with gypsies, cried "Govinda! Govinda!" in sacred Hindu temples, eaten ant egg soup in the east of Thailand and crossed a corner of the Sahara on her camel whose name was Bob Marley. When inspired, she blogs at https://dianewanderer.blogspot.com. Caldwell's award-winning stories have appeared in the anthologies: "Dancing My Way Home," *Tales From the Ex-pat Harem*; "Desert Queen," *Best Women's Travel Writing 2010*; and "The Guest," *Mambo Poa 2*. Her forthcoming works include "My Lovely Uturus," *My Body, My Self*; "The Road to Freedom," *No Such Thing as a Free Ride*. Her story "In Search of Duende" received the Best Memoir of 2011 from the *Solas Awards*. "Ankor Wat Pilgrimage," received Best Travel Story of the Year from *Amazing Travel Stories.com*, and "Desert Wedding," was awarded "Best Story of the Year" by *Synergise.com*.

HELEN CARSON started writing poetry in January 2007, when she was challenged by a friend, also a successful poet, to try her hand at poetry. Her work has been seen in several literary venues including *Mosaic, Main Channel Voices, Third Wednesday* and *Voices of Breast Cancer*, an anthology published by LaChance and available on Amazon. Following a 30 year career as an RN and then 10 years as a consultant to Native American Head Start programs, Ms. Carson is now retired and enjoys being home with her husband and cocker spaniel. She is pursuing her love of travel, photography, altered art and collage, antiquing and cross-stitch. She is active in her local art association and shows her work at local art shows in Southern California.

ADAM CHESHIRE is a writer living in Hillsborough, NC. He is currently at work on a collection of ultrashort nonfiction stories, *Two Ways to Tell a Secret*.

CASEY CLABOUGH is the author of his new memoir *Schooled: Life Lessons of a College Professor*, the novel *Confederado*, the travel memoir *The Warrior's Path: Reflections Along an Ancient Route*, a recently-published biography of southern writer George Garrett, and five scholarly books on southern and Appalachian writers, including *Inhabiting Contemporary Southern & Appalachian Literature: Region & Place in the 21st Century*. Clabough serves as editor of the literature section of the *Virginia Foundation for the Humanities' Encyclopedia Virginia* and as general editor of the literary journal *James Dickey Review*. His work has appeared in over seventy anthologies and magazines, including *Creative Nonfiction*, the *Sewanee Review*, and the *Virginia Quarterly Review*. Clabough's awards include the Bangladesh International Literary Award, an Artists Grant from the Brazilian Government, and several U.S.-based fellowships. He lives on a farm in Appomattox County, Virginia and serves as English Graduate

Director at Lynchburg College. His forthcoming books include an anthology of Civil War writing by Virginia women entitled *Women of War: Writing by Virginia Women Who Lived through the Civil War* (2014).

BETH LYNN CLEGG of Houston, Texas, is an octogenarian who began her writing career after retiring from other endeavors. She has been published in a variety of genre, including the anthology *Impact: An Anthology of Short Memoirs* (Telling Our Stories Press).

ELLEN DWORSKY is a California native who has lived in Israel, Italy, Brazil, and the foreign country of Minnesota, where she got her MFA in creative nonfiction. She now lives in Albuquerque, New Mexico. Her work has appeared in two anthologies: *Blink Again, Sudden Fiction From the Upper Midwest* and *A Cup of Comfort for Writers*, as well as various magazines and literary journals such as, *Minnesota Monthly, Rattle, The Truth About the Fact, Whistling Shade, Poetica, White Crow, Your Tango*, and many others.

MICHAEL ESTABROOK spent 40 years of working for "The Man" and sometimes "The Woman" and is finally free. No more useless meetings under florescent lights in stuffy windowless rooms. He concentrates instead on making better poems and on pursuing his other interests including: history, art, music, theatre, opera, and his wife who is still the most beautiful woman he has ever known.

KATHY GILBERT is an award-winning poet and is a 2013 MFA graduate from San Francisco State University. She previously worked in public transportation. Her poetry and translations have been published, or are forthcoming, in *The Squaw Valley Review, Transfer, Anomolous, Best of the Steel Toe Review*, and on line at *Swampwriting.com*. She is beginning to learn Mandarin and hopes to travel by high-speed train in China. She lives in Daly City, CA but grew up in Western New York.

CARMEN GILLESPIE is a professor of English, director of the Griot Institute for Africana Studies, and University Arts Coordinator at Bucknell University. In addition to article and poem publications, she is the author of the scholarly works *A Critical Companion to Toni Morrison* (2007), *A Critical Companion to Alice Walker* (2011), and the editor of *Toni Morrison: Forty Years in the Clearing* (2012). Carmen has also published a poetry chapbook, *Lining the Rails* (2008) and a poetry collection, *Jonestown: A Vexation*, which won the 2011 Naomi Long Madgett Poetry Prize. Carmen's awards include an Ohio Arts Council Individual Artist Fellowship for Excellence in Poetry and grants from the NEH, the Mellon Foundation, the Bread Loaf Writer's Conference, and the Fine Arts Work Center in Provincetown. She is a Cave Canem Fellow and a Fulbright scholar. *Essence* magazine named Carmen one of its 40 favorite poets in commemoration of the magazine's 40th anniversary.

RICHARD GOODMAN is the author of *French Dirt: The Story of a Garden in the South of France*. His other books are *The Soul of Creative Writing*, *A New York Memoir* and *The Bicycle Diaries: One New Yorker's Journey Through 9-11*. He has written for *The New York Times, Harvard Review, Creative Nonfiction, Commonweal, Vanity Fair, The Writer's Chronicle, The Louisville Review, Saveur, Ascent*, and the *Michigan Quarterly Review*. Richard is Assistant Professor of English at the University of New Orleans.

BOBBIE HAYSE mostly lives and writes in Bowling Green, Kentucky. She shares a home with three dudes; two of which are canine and the other, a homosexual homo-sapien. They recently purchased a grill, and are enjoying the zenith from their back porch as they cook delicious fish.

ASHLEY HENLEY is an editor living in the Washington, DC metro area with her husband, three dogs, and three cats. She is working on finishing her Master of Professional Writing and enjoys riding her pink scooter around town.

JESSICA HERIOT is a retired psychotherapist living in Hendersonville in Western North Carolina. She is writing a memoir about her "feminist career."

MEREDITH HOFFMAN is a writer and journalist currently living Brooklyn and working as a reporter for the news site *DNAinfo.com* (New York). A graduate of Cornell University with an M.A. in journalism from NYU, she has written articles that have appeared in the *New York Times, Huffington Post* and the *New York Observer.* She writes both fiction and poetry and has recently started a blog. (http://meredithhoffman.wordpress.com/)

JEAN HORAK lives in South Texas with her cat and guinea pig. She has a degree in Biomedical Sciences and works full time as a blood bank technologist. With the love of expressing oneself, Jean enjoys writing in her spare time as a way to keep the world from seeming so mundane.

STEPHANIE C. HORTON is a Liberian writer and editor living in exile in North America. Her children's book, *What Happened to Red Rooster When A Visitor Came,* is taught as a text in Liberian schools. She is a graduate of Spalding University's MFA program.

WILLIAM L. JANES is the end result of several different forces that at one point worked to corrode the armor that kept his very soul from decomposing. His reasons for the twenty-plus years spent plumbing the vicissitudes of human experience are what he lovingly refers to as "research," and are rich fodder for genealogists and addiction counselors alike. He lives in Northern Virginia with his lovely wife Conzuelo, and a tuxedo cat known as Misch.

MARILYN JUNE JANSON, M.S., Ed. teaches creative writing for the Maricopa Community Colleges in Phoenix, AZ. She is the owner of Janson Literary Services, Inc. Learn more about Ms. Janson at www.janwrite.com.

JAMIE JOHNSON is an antique/gift shop owner who enjoys writing about her fascinating children. Her full-length memoir *Secret Selves: How Their Changes Changed Me* won an IP Book Award for Best Non-fiction in Eastern Canada and was a finalist in the Beverly Hills Book Awards. Her short pieces have appeared in *The Globe & Mail, Homemakers Magazine, Brain, Child Magazine, Families in TRANSition* (a resource book for trans families) and the anthology, *Hidden Lives: Coming Out on Mental Illness*. She is currently working on her first novel.

CAROL KANTER is a psychotherapist in Evanston, IL. Her work has appeared in numerous literary journals and anthologies including *Ariel, Atlanta Review, Blue Unicorn, ByLine, Earth's Daughters, Evening Street Review, Explorations, Hammers, Iowa Woman, The Chester Jones Foundation, Kaleidoscope Ink, The Madison Review, Memoir (and), The Mid-America Poetry Review, Pudding Magazine, The People's Press, Rambunctious Review, River Oak Review, Sendero, Sweet Annie Press, Thema*, and *Universities West Press. Atlanta Review* gave her three International Merit Awards before publishing two of her poems. Finishing Line Press published her two chapbooks, *Out of Southern Africa* (2005) and

Chronicle of Dog (2006). *No Secret Where Elephants Walk* (2010) marries Carol's poetry to her husband's photography from Africa (www.DualArtsPress.com). Carol and her husband have two daughters.

EVELYN LAMPART is a retired clinical social worker, free to write and paint. She is a native New Yorker, born in Harlem in the fifties, and a witness to the constant changes taking place in the city, especially her borough of Brooklyn.

GINA MARIE LAZAR is a Philadelphia-based writer/artist. Her recent work has appeared in *CALYX Journal, Fringe Magazine, The Buddhist Poetry Review*, and *Tiferet Journal*. Find her art online at: www.virtuallygina.com and writings at: www.iridescently.wordpress.com

CATHERINE LEE spent her early years along the shores of Virginia before expatriating to a foreign country known as Texas. She is currently studying English literature, history, and education at Texas A&M University. She lives with her husband and two children.

JANINE LEHANE is from Brisbane, Australia and is a graduate of The College of William and Mary in Williamsburg, Virginia, where she was the coordinator of a statewide program for promising student authors. She now teaches in a M.Ed. program at Columbia College in South Carolina and lives in the Blue Ridge Mountains of Western North Carolina.

GERALD A. MCBREEN had the unique distinction of holding three Poet Laureate positions simultaneously. He was one of the winners of a contest sponsored by Amy Kitchener's Angels Without Wings and awarded the title of Senior Poet Laureate of Washington State (2012). In celebration of it's centennial year the city of Pacific appointed him their Poet Laureate (2009-2014). A few months later Auburn Morning Toastmasters honored him with the same title (2010-2014). McBreen discovered poetry after he retired from the U. S. Postal Service. He is published in *Gargoyle, Crab Creek Review, The Broome Review, ideals*, etc. McBreen says, "I never planned to be a poet. Poetry found me and wouldn't let go."

AILEEN R. MCCREADY obtained a B.A. in English with a concentration in writing from Loyola University in New Orleans. She has written for *Slidell Sentry-News* and *The Villages Daily Sun*. She also served as editor for *Why I Stayed*, an essay and photo project highlighting Hurricane Katrina survivors. She currently serves as membership coordinator for Writers Alliance of Gainesville in Gainesville, Florida.

LEOTA MCCOWN-HOOVER a semi-retired addictions/grief counselor lives in Arizona with her husband and two African Grey parrots. Her essays have appeared in *The Healing Muse, So to Speak, 2008 Byline Calendar, The Companion Parrot,* and *Threshold*.

CALLIE MELTON is a "spare time" writer living in Pineville, KY with her 6-year-old son. She is an Operations Administrator for Phillips Machine and has been the winner of several local writing contests over the past decade. She reads a lot and writes a little, mainly to amuse herself.

JASMINNE MENDEZ is a performance poet, actress, teacher and published writer. She received her B.A. in English Literature and M.Ed. in Curriculum and Instruction from the University of Houston. Mendez has performed her poetry in venues all around Houston, including the MFAH, Rice and the Alley Theatre. She has shared the stage with respected writers and poets, notably,

Sandra Cisneros and Taylor Mali. Mendez has been published both nationally and internationally and her first multi-genre memoir *Island of Dreams* was recently released by Floricanto Press.

E. ETHELBERT MILLER is a writer and literary activist. He was born in 1950 and grew-up in New York City. A graduate of Howard University, he was one of the first students at that institution to major in African American Studies. Today he is the board chair of the Institute for Policy Studies, a progressive think tank located in Washington, D.C. Miller is the director of the African American Resource Center at Howard University. He is editor of *Poet Lore*, the oldest poetry magazine published in the United States. In 1996, he was awarded an honorary degree of Doctor of Literature from Emory and Henry College. Mr. Miller has been a Fulbright Senior Specialist Program Fellow in 2004 and 2012. Miller is the founder and former chair of the Humanities Council of Washington, D.C. The author of several collections of poetry, he has also written two memoirs, *Fathering Words: The Making Of An African American Writer* (2000) and *The 5th Inning* (2009). *Fathering Words* was selected by the D.C. Public Library for its DC WE READ, one book, one city program in 2003. In 2013, *Fathering Words* will be released as an E book by Black Classic Press. Recently Mr. Miller began serving as host and producer of the television show *The Scholars* which airs on UDC-TV. In August 2012, he started writing *E ON DC*, a monthly newspaper column published by Capital Community News. Mr. Miller's poetry has been translated into Spanish, Portuguese, German, Hungarian, Chinese, Farsi, Norwegian, Tamil and Arabic. Mr. Miller has taught at UNLV, American University, George Mason University, and Emory and Henry College. For several years he was a core faculty member with the Bennington Writing Seminars. Mr. Miller is often heard on National Public Radio.

SUEANN PORTER lives in Upstate New York with her husband and a very spoiled dog named Bailey. Visit her blog http://www.sueannporter.wordpress.com/ where she talks about everyday real life occurrences, which are usually stranger than fiction. She is working on a book entitled *Short Spurts*.

DIANA RAAB is an award-winning poet, memoirist, blogger, writing instructor, inspirational speaker and author of eight books, including two memoirs, *Regina's Closet: Finding My Grandmother's Secret Journal* and *Healing With Words: A Writer's Cancer Journey*. She's editor of two anthologies, *Writers and Their Notebooks* and *Writers on the Edge: 22 Writers Speak About Addiction and Dependency*. She has four poetry collections: *Listening to Africa, Dear Anais: My Life in Poems for You, The Guilt Gene* and *My Muse Undresses Me*. Her fifth book of poetry, *Lust*, will be released in 2014. She's on the board of a number of literary organizations. She facilitates writing workshops around the country and teaches in the Antioch University Summer Writing Institute in Santa Barbara. She has been writing since the age of 10 when her mother gave her a journal, to help her cope with her grandmother's suicide. She's a regular blogger on the Huffington Post: http://www.huffingtonpost.com/diana-m-raab. She is currently working on her doctorate in psychology and studying the healing power of writing. Her website is www.dianaraab.com.

LORI ROTTENBERG lives in the Washington, DC area, and her poetry has been published in several journals, including *Artemis, Potomac Review*, and *Poetica*. Lori has also been a visiting poet for Arlington County Public Schools since 2007.

W. CLAYTON SCOTT was recently awarded the Governor's Art Award of Arkansas (2012) and was Poet Laureate of Fayetteville,

Arkansas. Scott is the author and performer of the one-person play, *Down in Littletown*. He holds a Masters of Fine Arts in Writing in Poetry and is the author of volumes of poetry, including *Mind Your Head* and *Sex and Other Matters of Regard*. He has ranked in the top ten percent of slam poets in the world and represented Arkansas in the National Poetry Slams. He has won numerous awards for his poetry. He was chosen as a poetry ambassador with the Arkansas Arts in Education program and is the founder of Student Poetry Movement. Clayton worked as a comedian for more than 20 years; and he taught school in Oklahoma before becoming a television producer for a local and nationally syndicated TV talk show. Clayton serves as a part of three Arkansas Arts Council programs. He is an avid photographer with an eye for unusual and common images. Learn more about his poetry, plays and photography at www.ClaytonScott.com

DON SEGAL of Guilford, CT, has been published in the *Deep Waters* anthology by the Tall Grass Writers Guild and in the *Emily Dickinson Poetry Award* (Universities West Press) anthology as a semi-finalist. Other publication credits include *Miriam's Well, Bottle Rockets, The Small Pond Magazine, Hummingbird* and *Blueline*. His poetry, landscape photography and drawings can be seen at www.donsegal.wordpress.com.

JUDITH SERIN teaches literature and creative writing at California College of the Arts and lives in San Francisco with her husband, Herbert Yee. Serin's collection of poetry, *Hiding in the World*, was published by Diane di Prima's Eidolon Editions, and her *Days Without (Sky): A Poem Tarot*, seventy-eight short prose poems in the form of a tarot deck with illustration and book art design by Nikki Thompson, was published by Deconstructed Artichoke Press. She writes fiction as well as poetry, and her work has appeared in numerous magazines and anthologies, including *Bachy, The Ohio Journal, Writer's Forum, Nebraska Review, Woman's World, Colorado State Review*, and *Barnabe Mountain Review*. Most recently she has published prose poems/memoirs in the anthologies *Proposing on the Brooklyn Bridge* (Grayson Books), *When Last on the Mountain* (Holy Cow! Press), and *Impact* (Telling Our Stories Press); in the journals *The Paterson Literary Review, First Intensity, Paragraph*, and *the blink*; and in a chapbook of nine prose poems, *Family Stories* (Deconstructed Artichoke Press).

ELAINE DUGAS SHEA is a New England native, has lived in Montana for 40 years, but still misses the ocean. She enjoyed a career in social justice working with American Indian Tribes and Civil Rights. Her writing was featured in *Third Wednesday, South Dakota Review*, the anthology *The Light in Ordinary Things*, the anthology *Hope Whispers, Samsara, Front Range Review, CAMAS, Spillway*, the anthology *When Last on the Mountain: The View from Writers over Fifty* and elsewhere.

MISSI SMITH is a teacher and writer on a constant quest to find the extraordinary in every day life, to live her life with intention, and to do some literary narrative along the way. She lives in the foothills of the North Cascade Mountains where she enjoys skiing, hiking, biking, and being surrounded by the inspiration of nature.

DIANE SPODAREK was awarded an NEA and three NYFA artists' fellowship grants. Publications include: *KGB Lit Magazine*, "Young Women's Monologues," and "Grisley Shorts" horror anthology. Her one-person show *The Drunk Monologues* was produced by BATS Theatre in New Zealand, Horse Trade Theatre in NY and The Fringe Festivals in NY & NZ. She was awarded "Poet of the Year" by *Downtown Magazine* and was the The First Runner Up at the First Grand Poetry Slam, Nuyorican Poets Café, NYC. She blogs at Dangerousdiane@blogspot.com

EMILY FRASER VOIGT has written for several b2b magazines, mostly covering technology trends on Wall Street. She has also done a lot of corporate writing and editing. She speaks French, German, a little Spanish, and has traveled more than most, but not as much as she would like. Originally from the UK, she currently lives in Brooklyn, New York.

PAVELLE WESSER resides in New England with her family and several dogs. Her fiction has appeared in ezines such as *Eclecticism, Paragraph Planet* and *Burning Word*. She is published in a *Frightmares* anthology by Stan Swanson, as well as Kimberly Raiser's *66 Twisted Tales in 66 Words*. Her work also appears in *100 Horrors: Tales of Horror in the Blink of an Eye*, by Kevin Bufton as well as in several anthologies by Wicked East Press.

CHANGMING YUAN is a 4-time Pushcart nominee and author of Allen Qing Yuan, holds a PhD in English, teaches privately and edits *Poetry Pacific* in Vancouver. Yuan's poetry appears in 639 literary publications across 24 countries, including *Barrow Street, Best Canadian Poetry* (2009, 2012), *BestNewPoemsOnline, Exquisite Corpse* and *London Magazine*.

SALLY ZAKARIYA is a writer whose poems and articles have appeared in numerous journals. A collection of her poems, *Arithmetic And Other Verses From Late In Life*, was published in 2011 by Richer Resources Publications. She won first and second place prizes in the Poetry Society of Virginia's 2013 poetry contest and has self-published illustrated alphabet books on food, literature, and anatomy. Sally lives in Arlington, Virginia, and blogs at www.butdoesitrhyme.com.

ABOUT THE EDITOR

As a lifetime diarist, CoCo Harris is drawn to personal narratives. For years she has guided others with crafting personal narratives through creative writing workshops and various memoir projects and publications.

Her story began in Atlanta, GA, and has traversed the Washington DC Metro area; Nigeria, West Africa: Seattle, WA; Louisville, KY; The Coast of Georgia; and Pennsylvania's Susquehanna Valley. Though she now lives in central PA, CoCo is particularly at home anywhere sun and surf meet.

She earned a B.S. in Electrical Engineering at Howard University, did graduate work in African Studies, and began her Intellectual Property Law career working for the Patent and Trademark Office while becoming a wife and a mother of three daughters. She later entered the US Patent Bar becoming a patent law professional wherein she represents individuals, firms, and corporations in the US and internationally.

She received her Master of Fine Arts in Writing in Fiction from Spalding University, and is a Zora Neale Hurston/Richard Wright Foundation alumna. She is the Founding Editor of Telling Our Stories Press. CoCo Harris is constantly exploring the notion of how we tell the stories of our lives with both fiction and nonfiction.

30304243R00073

Made in the USA
Charleston, SC
10 June 2014